25 Websi
Will Pay You
to Write

By Writing Axis

"A great resource for writers who need regular work that pays well."
— HBC Book Reviews

A BRIEF INTRODUCTION

The rise of the gig economy has provided more opportunities for writers to profit while working remotely. Whether you're looking to launch a writing career, supplement your income or increase your earning potential by writing for **high-paying, big-name** brands, this resource can help.

Includes:

- 25 websites that provide regular work for writers
- Sites that pay up to **$800 per article, $70 per hour** and $1.75 per word
- In-depth overviews providing insight into each opportunity
- Links to the websites, so you can easily apply

Perfect for:

- Established freelancers who want to earn big by writing for large brands
- Full-time writers in search of regular remote work
- People looking to earn extra income, build a portfolio and establish a writing career
- People with writing skills who want to supplement their income with well-paying part-time work

Other books by Writing Axis:

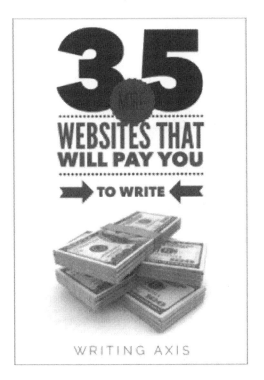

35 *More*
Websites that
Will Pay You to Write

Get even more. Thirty-five extra sites that will pay you up to $1,500 per article.
New to writing? An experienced pro? This honest, informative book will help you take the next step in you work-from-home writing career.

Download from Amazon here

TABLE OF CONTENTS

LIST OF 25 PAYING WEBSITES

#1

Content Bacon

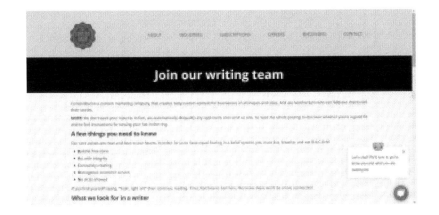

Overview

ContentBacon a digital marketing business that creates custom content for businesses of all shapes and sizes.

From a writer's perspective, ContentBacon provides opportunities to earn money writing for some very big brands. Of course, ContentBacon takes a cut, but there's still some very good money left over.

This is a good opportunity for new writers and experienced professional writers who need to supplement their existing client base. It's also a good option for people who need to supplement their income with a reliable work-from-home job.

DIGGING DEEPER INTO BACON

What Bacon looks for in writers:

Curiosity: People who write for Bacon have to do a of research. And they are good at it. They read a lot and stay up to date on all the best practices. They like digging into unfamiliar topics and quickly become experts in the subject matter.

Storytellers: Bacon writers know that each piece of fresh content—each social post, blog, whitepaper, newsletter and video script is basically a short story within a bigger brand story. They see the bigger picture and can reduce it into easily digestible segments.

Good editors: Bacon likes writers who strive for impeccability. They want people who will take the time to critique and review their work before they submit it to make sure that every piece supports the client's strategy. They also want writers who will optimize content for both people and SEO.

Conversion-centric: Bacon wants writers who understand the time-honored art of persuasion and can provide subtle, clever and effective copy. They like writers who understand that content should not be a hard sell, but an invitation to feel, think and act. (TIP: If you do not know who Joanna Wiebe is, read about her before applying.)

Open to feedback: Bacon wants writers who are open to self-improvement. They need to be able to take on feedback from our editors and clients. When work gets sent back for revisions, writers need to view it, not a failure, but as a challenge.

Versatility: Bacon looks for writers who are natural mimics. In essence, they want writers who can absorb a brand's unique personality and take on its style, voice and tone. In some instances, they even ask writers to create a brand's voice.

Strategic: Bacon is interested in writers who understand strategy and branding. Instead of merely taking orders, writers need to be able to collaborate with our Bacon's editors to develop content that people really want to read. They may also be asked to actively suggest ideas for client blogs based on research. If an assignment feels entirely off-base, writers are asked to have a conversation with the editor before they attempt to write it to ensure it is in alignment with the overall content strategy.

Communicative and Deadline-driven: When guidance is needed or information is lacking, Bacon asks writers to speak up and ask for support. They don't want writers who wallow in misery or get lured down the rabbit hole. If a deadline is looming and they aren't not sure they will meet it, writers need to speak up and be proactive. They must let the editors know it may not happen as soon as they hoped and there is a potential issue. They will also be asked to set a new expectation for when they will be able to have it done. This will allow Bacon's editors to communicate with clients or reassign content with a hard deadline in enough time for another writer to complete the task.

What Bacon expects from writers

- They take the time to visit each client's website and familiarize themselves with their market and business.
- They review the client's intake questionnaire, the client's blog and any resources Bacon provides.
- They visit competitors to see what they are doing and discover ways to do it better.
- They understand SEO basics and how to incorporate keyword phrases into each article, while always writing for humans first.
- They link out to the customer's other blog and landing pages whenever it relates to the content they are writing.
- They make sure everything they write is in line with each client's brand and tailored toward their target audience.
- They welcome constructive criticism from the client and senior team members.
- They are willing to revise articles when necessary based on client feedback.

- They turn things in quickly and willingly take on projects with strict deadlines.
- They don't look at the things they do for clients as an assignment; Bacon only wants writers who want to tell stories and create compelling content -- not simply finish tasks as they come up.

They have a "whatever it takes" perspective and really want to impress clients with their writing and creative abilities.

Get the details about Content Bacon at:

https://writingaxis.com/content-bacon/

Note: We encourage writers to carefully read through this site's posted publishing requirements, submission guidelines and unique payment policy. Although we always vet each outlet we include in our listings; certain sites are better suited for experienced freelance writers who have impressive portfolios and lots of experience. That said, other sites are better suited for less experienced writers who need to build up their portfolios, recent college graduates, people who need extra income, and experienced freelance writers who need to make a living in between gigs.

If this website or another website on our list alters or updates their posted publishing requirements, submission guidelines or unique payment policies; we will respond by updating this listing as soon as possible. If you have knowledge of any helpful info, please feel free to contact us at hr@writingaxis.com.

#2

Quietly

Overview

Quietly is a leading digital marketing agency that creates, distributes and monetizes written content for some of the world's biggest brands.

The agency connects writers with publishers and brands, based on their qualifications, expertise and preferred interests.

If you're approved, they will place you in their database. Whenever they have an available new project, the company searches the database for an available writer. You can make good money with Quietly, but it's generally best to use the agency to supplement your other work. If you use it with two or three other sites in this resource, you should stay pretty busy and be able to make a good living.

DIGGING DEEPER INTO QUIETLY

How to become a writer at Quietly:

When they have new projects, Quietly will search its database for an available candidate. To get in the database, you need to visit the site and:

1 Tell them about yourself
Fill out a Quietly writer profile so they can get a sense of your expertise and interests.

2 Show them your work
Add several writing samples (white papers, articles, etc.) and showcase your writing abilities. If you don't have any published writing samples, we recommend Portfolio Right Now.

3 Get matched
Whenever a writing opportunity comes up that matches your interests and skill set, Quietly will get in touch.

4 Wait for your brief
Quietly will send you a brief that details content requirements and includes info about the brand's target audience and style guide.

5 Receive feedback
You will collaborate with Quietly's editors to receive guidance and create engaging stories.

6 Invoice Quietly and get paid
As soon as your work is complete and ready to publish, you can invoice us Quietly. They'll process your payment within about 30 days.

You will find Quietly's submission details at:

https://writingaxis.com/quiet-ly/

Note: We encourage writers to carefully read through this site's posted publishing requirements, submission guidelines and unique payment policy. Although we always vet each outlet we include in our listings; certain sites are better suited for experienced freelance writers who have impressive portfolios and lots of experience. That said, other sites are better suited for less experienced writers who need to build up their portfolios, recent college graduates, people who need extra income, and experienced freelance writers who need to make a living in between gigs.

If this website or another website on our list alters or updates their posted publishing requirements, submission guidelines or unique payment policies; we will respond by updating this listing as soon as possible. If you have knowledge of any helpful info, please feel free to contact us at hr@writingaxis.com.

#3

ClearVoice

Overview

Somewhat like a writer's mill, ClearVoice is designed to create a collaborative workspace, which lets companies secure the services of freelance writers.

When you sign up, you are joining a talent network and will ne matched with assignments based on your expertise and rate. Once you add a CV and portfolio, companies will be able to send you work based on your abilities and specified minimum rate. You can also pitch ideas to clients.

With ClearVoice, you set your own rates, which could be anything from 10 cents per word or $1 per word. The lower your rate, the more offers you will get. That said, you can decline any offer if it doesn't suit your schedule, strengths or interests.

DIGGING DEEPER INTO CLEARVOICE

ClearVoice fancies itself as "an entrepreneurial ladder" more than a freelance job.

Its collaborative workspace and Talent Network allow freelancers and in-house editorial teams to seamlessly collaborate. The company's stated goal is to help writers seize opportunities and deliver their best work — with less hassle and less hustle.

With ClearVoice, you can build your personal brand.

If you are serious about freelance writing as a career, ClearVoice can help you strengthen your CV Portfolio and grow your business.

Secure Better Jobs

With an enhanced CV, you can join ClearVoice's Talent Network, where assignments are matched by expertise, past writing samples and rate. You also even pitch to clients in some instances.

Share Your CV Portfolio

The company is constantly improving its CVs (ClearVoice portfolios), so writers can better showcase their work and attract more clients. Again, if you don't have any published writing samples, and want to land bigger clients right away, we recommend Portfolio Right Now.

Set Your Own Rate

ClearVoice allows you to decide what you want to charge. Set your range to view assignments relevant to you and your rate.

Easily Communicate with Clients

ClearVoice offers in-app messaging that lets you to chat with clients during the creation process. This results in fewer emails and time-consuming edits.

Get Paid Quickly

ClearVoice pays freelancers via PayPal once assignments are approved by the client. You can work with the confidence you will get paid on time.

Get the details about the ClearVoice talent network at:

https://writingaxis.com/clearvoice-2/

Note: We encourage writers to carefully read through this site's posted publishing requirements, submission guidelines and unique payment policy. Although we always vet each outlet we include in our listings; certain sites are better suited for experienced freelance writers who have impressive portfolios and lots of experience. That said, other sites are better suited for less experienced writers who need to build up their portfolios, recent college graduates, people who need extra income, and experienced freelance writers who need to make a living in between gigs.

If this website or another website on our list alters or updates their posted publishing requirements, submission guidelines or unique payment policies; we will respond by updating this listing as soon as possible. If you have knowledge of any helpful info, please feel free to contact us at hr@writingaxis.com.

#4

Constant Content

Overview

Constant Content is a good place to make decent money online, whether you're a seasoned professional writer or a new writer just starting out.

With this platform, you can earn one of two ways: You can upload your articles or blog posts and make them available for sale. You set the price, and if someone is interested, they will buy either full or partial rights to the content depending on your preference.

The second method involves the public request area, where businesses ask for specific types of content. You can then write the content and submit it for consideration. If the requester likes it, they will purchase it; if they don't, or someone beats you to the punch, you can always put the piece up for sale to other buyers.

DIGGING DEEPER INTO CONSTANT CONTENT

Constant Content is trusted by countless top businesses including Zulily, Uber, The Home Depot, Hayneedle, Walgreens, CVS, eBay and many others. It's one of the largest and most established writing platforms for facilitating connections between writers and big brands.

Now, you should understand that this site can be frustrating at times. Until you get used to the way it works, it's generally best to submit your existing work for purchase and only claim the occasional project you are sure you can do well. Once you get the gist, you can start getting a bit more aggressive.

Start by Creating your profile

Create a professional bio that will showcase your writing experience and skill set.

Apply for some projects

Browse available projects and claim writing jobs that match your expertise, interests and rate.

Connect with big brands

Connect with top brands, so you can build long-term relationships. While Constant Content frowns on this, big brands will contact you with more work on the side if you do a great job.

Advance your career

Keep writing content, earn money, grow your portfolio, cultivate relationships and advance your career as a writer.

Get details about Constant Content at:

https://writingaxis.com/constant-content-2/

Note: We encourage writers to carefully read through this site's posted publishing requirements, submission guidelines and unique payment policy. Although we always vet each outlet we include in our listings; certain sites are better suited for experienced freelance writers who have impressive portfolios and lots of experience. That said, other sites are better suited for less experienced writers who need to build up their portfolios, recent college graduates, people who need extra income, and experienced freelance writers who need to make a living in between gigs.

If this website or another website on our list alters or updates their posted publishing requirements, submission guidelines or unique payment policies; we will respond by updating this listing as soon as possible. If you have knowledge of any helpful info, please feel free to contact us at hr@writingaxis.com.

#5

eByline

Overview

eByline is a part of the Izea brand, which connects online influencers with major brands.

If you have a social media profile with a lot of followers, Izea can help you monetize your account by posting about products. If not, that's ok; you can still get paid to write custom content for top brands, publishers, advertisers and ecommerce companies.

To do this, you will need to join the creator marketplace full of freelance projects for writers, journalists, photographers, videographers, animators, designers, musicians and composers. Freelancer pay at eByline is all over the chart, but you can expect to make a very good income if you decide to stick with it.

DIGGING DEEPER INTO EBYLINE

eByline allows you to

Monetize your creativity, content and influence in one of the largest marketplaces of its kind.

You Bring the Passion, They Bring the Brands

Start by creating a free profile for an opportunity to partner with industry-leading fashion, food, lifestyle and beauty brands.

Monetize your writing and influence in the industry's biggest social media influencer marketplace. Connect with advertisers, brands and publishers for all sorts of sponsorship opportunities to develop and share content across your individual social media accounts in exchange for money.

Get paid for creating custom content for top advertisers, brands, publishers, and ecommerce businesses. Join the creator marketplace to access freelance opportunities for writers, journalists, photographers, videographers, animators, designers, musicians and composers.

Get details about eByline and the Izea brand at:

https://writingaxis.com/ebyline-2/

Note: We encourage writers to carefully read through this site's posted publishing requirements, submission guidelines and unique payment policy. Although we always vet each outlet we include in our listings; certain sites are better suited for experienced freelance writers who have impressive portfolios and lots of experience. That said, other sites are better suited for less experienced writers who need to build up their portfolios, recent college graduates, people who need extra income, and experienced freelance writers who need to make a living in between gigs.

If this website or another website on our list alters or updates their posted publishing requirements, submission guidelines or unique payment policies; we will respond by updating this listing as soon as possible. If you have knowledge of any helpful info, please feel free to contact us at hr@writingaxis.com.

#6

nDash

Overview

A relatively new brand, nDash works much like other content providers which seek to earn commission-like fees for linking talent with brands

At this point, the idea should sound familiar: nDash recruits a large pool of writers and makes them available to brands. The businesses then choose the writers for projects, and nDash takes a cut of the pay.

If you join the nDash writers pool, you will have the chance to write for thousands of brands of all sizes and industries. You will get paid promptly for each completed assignment, while having a chance to develop real relationships with major brands.

Could this lead to an in-house opportunity with a big company? Perhaps. But in the meantime, nDash allows you to profit by project. Since you can set your own rates for assignments, it's easy to experiment with numbers to see which rate brings you the most work.

DIGGING DEEPER INTO NDASH

They Want Elite Writers

nDash offers higher rates, opportunities from legitimate brands, and six-figure earning potential.

They Have Great Clients

nDash has partnerships with thousands of well-known brands of all sizes, niches and industries — and they are all searching for great writers.

They Offer Fast Payments

nDash writers are paid with every completed project, and no fees are subtracted from your earnings.

They Provide Full Transparency

nDash puts writers in direct communication with clients so they can build real, long-term relationships.

They Offer Big Earning Potential

In addition to paid projects, nDash offers lifetime royalties for any successful company referral.

They Connect You with Top Brands

nDash brands seek the most experienced, talented, experienced and creative writers (not the cheapest). With nDash, you can pitch unique ideas for articles and blog posts to showcase your expertise.

You Can Set Your Rates

Instead of starting off with an arbitrary low rating that earns you two cents per word; nDash allows you to set your own pay rates for assignments.

They Are Open and Transparent

While other platforms restrict communication, nDash puts you in contact with companies for every assignment so you can cultivate real relationships.

You Can Leverage Your Expertise

Brands on nDash are searching for writers with real subject matter expertise. You should tailor your profile to focus on the industries, categories and topics that interest you most.

Get the guidelines and details about nDash at:

https://writingaxis.com/ndash-2/

Note: We encourage writers to carefully read through this site's posted publishing requirements, submission guidelines and unique payment policy. Although we always vet each outlet we include in our listings; certain sites are better suited for experienced freelance writers who have impressive portfolios and lots of experience. That said, other sites are better suited for less experienced writers who need to build up their portfolios, recent college graduates, people who need extra income, and experienced freelance writers who need to make a living in between gigs.

If this website or another website on our list alters or updates their posted publishing requirements, submission guidelines or unique payment policies; we will respond by updating this listing as soon as possible. If you have knowledge of any helpful info, please feel free to contact us at hr@writingaxis.com.

#7

Contently

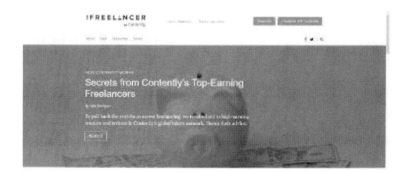

Overview

Contently is one of the world's largest enterprise content marketing platforms, creative networks and content strategy services.

Through the platform, freelance writers have an opportunity to work with top brands on high-quality projects that pay well. How well? This can vary, but a good project will usually pay at least $1 per word.

Once they register with Contently, writers are matched with brands. They can then pitch ideas, submit work and instantly receive payment all in one place. To become eligible for work, writers have to join the network by creating a free portfolio that will showcase their projects and professional expertise.

DIGGING DEEPER INTO CONTENTLY

Contently has created a platform that lets writers and creatives showcase their talents in a way that's user-friendly for businesses and freelancers. You can update a portfolio or reel with just a few clicks and connect with new prospective clients rather seamlessly.

Match with big clients

With Contently, freelancers are assigned projects based on whether their individual portfolios match a client's unique needs. The company works with brands across numerous industries, especially in the areas of travel, healthcare, finance and enterprise technology.

Collaborate on diverse projects

Once you are assigned to a client's team, you will be able to accept assignment briefs and pitch projects to editors. You can also work on everything from case studies and reported stories to photoshoots, infographics and video productions.

Get paid fast

Once you submit your work, Contently will credit you with a payment in your account. As soon as it appears, you can cash out to your individual PayPal account.

Repeat

The more deadlines you meet, content you pitch and stories you tell, the more Contently and its clients pay attention. That means you will be top-of-mind when clients come looking for a skilled contributor.

Get details about writing for Contently at:

https://writingaxis.com/contently-2/

Note: We encourage writers to carefully read through this site's posted publishing requirements, submission guidelines and unique payment policy. Although we always vet each outlet we include in our listings; certain sites are better suited for experienced freelance writers who have impressive portfolios and lots of experience. That said, other sites are better suited for less experienced writers who need to build up their portfolios, recent college graduates, people who need extra income, and experienced freelance writers who need to make a living in between gigs.

If this website or another website on our list alters or updates their posted publishing requirements, submission guidelines or unique payment policies; we will respond by updating this listing as soon as possible. If you have knowledge of any helpful info, please feel free to contact us at hr@writingaxis.com.

#8

Writer Access

Overview

If you're looking for high pay, Writer Access isn't going to be your best option. A writer can only expect to make between $.014 and $.07 per word. What's more, you have to prove your worth by submitting consistent quality work before you will be allowed to claim higher-paying projects.

With that said, the platform does provide regular work which can keep you busy if you're looking to make some extra money or build up your portfolio. It also provides opportunities for editors, translators and content strategists. These jobs start at approximately $21 each near the bottom. If you work your way up, however, you can claim projects that pay up to $70 per hour.

Just like most writer's mills, Writer's Access has its drawbacks. It can be useful, however, if you need to get some experience, build up a lackluster portfolio or make ends meet while you look for a higher-paying opportunity.

DIGGING DEEPER INTO WRITER ACCESS

Writer Access centers on the idea that remote work is now the mainstream. It's mainly interested in remote part-time and full-time writers that can provide personalized service, exceptional solutions and good content for its ever-growing list of corporate clients.

Each writer is expected to represent the company's brand, driven by individual, company and department goals -- all tied to generous bonuses.

You will need to fill out an application to get approved for an account at Writer Access. Send them you very best writing samples, spanning more than one topic. If you don't have any published writing samples, we recommend Portfolio Right Now.

You will find Writer Access's submission details at:

https://writingaxis.com/writer-access-2/

Note: We encourage writers to carefully read through this site's posted publishing requirements, submission guidelines and unique payment policy. Although we always vet each outlet we include in our listings; certain sites are better suited for experienced freelance writers who have impressive portfolios and lots of experience. That said, other sites are better suited for less experienced writers who need to build up their portfolios, recent college graduates, people who need extra income, and experienced freelance writers who need to make a living in between gigs.

If this website or another website on our list alters or updates their posted publishing requirements, submission guidelines or unique payment policies; we will respond by updating this listing as soon as possible. If you have knowledge of any helpful info, please feel free to contact us at hr@writingaxis.com.

#9

Cracked

Articles

Overview

Another pay-per-piece outlet, Cracked pays for humorous lists, articles and photos.

The outlet pays hundreds of dollars for every accepted piece. Although you shouldn't expect to make a regular income with this publisher; if your content is accepted, it will be seen by millions of people.

The outlet has some pretty stringent rules and guidelines, so be sure to thoroughly read over each one before submitting your content.

DIGGING DEEPER INTO CRACKED

If you are a smart, funny, creative writer, Cracked is the very best outlet for your talent.

No experience is necessary. The site will pay you if it's good, no questions asked. You talk directly to the editors, and they give a thumb up or down.

If your work gets approved, it could be seen by millions of viewers. Cracked is very interested in not just writers and artists, but people who can do a little bit of both.

To get paid for the list-style feature articles Cracked is famous for, you just need to sign up for the website's writers' forum. The only thing they require is that you demonstrate that you are creative, passionate and respectful of all the other writers. Basically, it takes nearly zero effort to join.

If you'd rather write bite-sized comedy content, Cracked is always looking for writers to create informative, entertaining images that are sharable on social media.

One of the most popular comedy sites in the world, Cracked will expose your content to countless people. That said, they are very, very picky about what they publish on the front page. Still, they will give virtually anyone a chance. If you are good, you will get paid.

Get details about writing for Chicken Soup for the Soul at:

https://writingaxis.com/cracked/

Note: We encourage writers to carefully read through this site's posted publishing requirements, submission guidelines and unique payment policy. Although we always vet each outlet we include in our listings; certain sites are better suited for experienced freelance writers who have impressive portfolios and lots of experience. That said, other sites are better suited for less experienced writers who need to build up their portfolios, recent college graduates, people who need extra income, and experienced freelance writers who need to make a living in between gigs.

If this website or another website on our list alters or updates their posted publishing requirements, submission guidelines or unique payment policies; we will respond by updating this listing as soon as possible. If you have knowledge of any helpful info, please feel free to contact us at hr@writingaxis.com.

#10

Link-Able

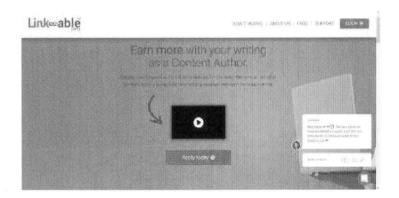

Overview

Link-Able allows writers to earn money publishing for a wide range of clients and industries.

The platform matches writers who are able to publish on relevant sites with companies looking to earn mentions, links and traffic to their sites.

Link-Able offers $100 to $750 per piece depending on the sites you either have authorship on or are able to successfully pitch to. Niches include business, marketing, finance, health, sport, tech, retail and more.

To earn money with this website, you will need to be able to write good content and get it published at relevant blogs and websites. Still, even if you are only able to publish one to three articles per month, that could add an extra $300 to $2,100 to your income.

DIGGING DEEPER INTO LINK-ABLE

With Link-able, you can find link building jobs and increase your earnings as a professional freelance writer.

Step 1 - You are a talented writer who enjoys writing and is able to guest blog for sites within your preferred niche.

Step 2 - Join Link-able and then search for content you think you will be able to link to within your next article. You will only find quality content that will make great links.

Step 3 - Relevantly incorporate the link into your article; then publish the article as a guest author on a website.

Step 4 - Get paid for each single link you are able to add within your article from Link-able.

Earn more with your freelance writing

Freelance writers typically don't get paid enough for their work. With Link-able, you are able to increase your writing revenue without having to write additional content. You get paid - not just for writing - but for adding relevant backlinks within your articles to sources you choose.

You can earn between $100 to $750 for every link you add, and you can add as many potential links as you are able to. Many of Link-able's Content Authors earn more than $1000 in additional revenue just for one article.

You can search Link-able and choose only the content you would like to link to. Link-able only allows websites with unique, high-quality content, so you always have reputable choices to link to.

Pick with common topics you are already working on

There is no need to write fresh content about a topic you don't care about. Simply search Link-able to find reputable content you can link to that is already related to the topic you're writing.

Grow your portfolio and writing career

Link-able allows freelance writers to go out and make a name for themselves. We want you to use your byline and publish your work around the web. With Link-able, you can develop your author portfolio and get paid for writing high-quality articles you will be proud to share with employers.

Get details about writing for Link-Able at:

https://writingaxis.com/link-able-2/

Note: We encourage writers to carefully read through this site's posted publishing requirements, submission guidelines and unique payment policy. Although we always vet each outlet we include in our listings; certain sites are better suited for experienced freelance writers who have impressive portfolios and lots of experience. That said, other sites are better suited for less experienced writers who need to build up their portfolios, recent college graduates, people who need extra income, and experienced freelance writers who need to make a living in between gigs.

If this website or another website on our list alters or updates their posted publishing requirements, submission guidelines or unique payment policies; we will respond by updating this listing as soon as possible. If you have knowledge of any helpful info, please feel free to contact us at hr@writingaxis.com.

#11

Funds for Writers

Overview

FundsforWriters pays for practical articles aimed at helping writers get paid for their writing.

They have a preference for success stories, but informative pieces sell well too as long as they are well-researched.

You can expect to make from $45 to $50 per article, depending on whether you want to be paid via PayPal or by check. Articles are usually accepted within a week of submission.

DIGGING DEEPER INTO FUNDS FOR WRITERS

Freelance Submission for FundsforWriters

FundsforWriters wants articles with word counts between 500 and 600. Every FundsforWriters newsletter will list just one article, brief and right to the point; so, it's important to make every word count. Always make your writing tight and avoid the passive voice at all costs. Give it a beginning, a nice middle and solid ending. A list of links is not considered an article.

They only want articles about making a living as a writer.

FundsforWriters does NOT want stories about:

- How to write
- How to develop characters, plots or settings
- Topics that can't relate in some way to earning more money as a writer
- Theoretical content anything without solid resources and examples

FundsforWriters DOES want stories about:

- Ideas on breaking into a specific writing markets (avoid naming vendors or publications
- Pointers on winning paying writing contests
- Grant success stories
- Clever ways to earn an income with writing
- Success stories about working as a writer with advice for others
- Profitable business practices that relate to writing
- Seasonal material affiliated with certain markets
- Nonprofit partnerships for professional writers
- Unique paying markets for writers
- Unusual or unique writing income ideas

- Anything that can help a writer make money
- A little humor, a positive note and a happy ending, when appropriate

If you suggest a topic, make sure you provide proof it actually works through your own experience or interviews with other writers.

Payment: Via check – They rarely pay via check and never outside the United States.

PayPal – FundsforWriters pays $50 for unpublished unique articles; $15 for reprints.

Get details about writing for Funds for Writers at:

https://writingaxis.com/funds-for-writers-2/

Note: We encourage writers to carefully read through this site's posted publishing requirements, submission guidelines and unique payment policy. Although we always vet each outlet we include in our listings; certain sites are better suited for experienced freelance writers who have impressive portfolios and lots of experience. That said, other sites are better suited for less experienced writers who need to build up their portfolios, recent college graduates, people who need extra income, and experienced freelance writers who need to make a living in between gigs.

If this website or another website on our list alters or updates their posted publishing requirements, submission guidelines or unique payment policies; we will respond by updating this listing as soon as possible. If you have knowledge of any helpful info, please feel free to contact us at hr@writingaxis.com.

#12

Skyword

Overview

Skyword brands itself as specializing in "The art and science of content marketing." What this really means is the company serves clients in search of agency-style content marketing.

From a writer's perspective, Skyword provides opportunities to earn money writing for some very big brands. Of course, Skyword takes a cut, but there's still some very good money left over after. At Skyword, writers can earn from $150 to $800 per article, especially if you can provide good ghostwriting and tech content.

Skyword has two ways of operating: They offer the full-service setup for clients where they plan a specific content strategy, set the writer's pay rate, and act as intermediary between the client and writer.

Skyword also allows companies to search its writer pool and select writers. Whatever the case, there are big opportunities if you can earn a place in the Skyword writers pool.

DIGGING DEEPER INTO SKYWORD

Skyword connects exceptional graphic designers, writers, photographers, videographers and other creatives with the world's biggest brands who want to connect with their audiences through effective storytelling.

An Elite Community of Creatives

Skyword's contributor community is a big reason why its clients trust the company to develop and deliver their branded stories. They review each portfolio in detail to make sure its community is only comprised of the very best of the best.

The platform handles scheduling, assignments and payment, so writers (and other creatives) can concentrate on doing what they do best.

Elite Writers, Top Brands

Join Skyword for the opportunity to do some of the very best work of your career for the world's biggest brands. Skyword is constantly growing, and its customers are constantly searching for talented freelancers who specialize in a wide array of areas.

Get the guidelines and details about Skyword at:

https://writingaxis.com/skyword-2/

Note: We encourage writers to carefully read through this site's posted publishing requirements, submission guidelines and unique payment policy. Although we always vet each outlet we include in our listings; certain sites are better suited for experienced freelance writers who have impressive portfolios and lots of experience. That said, other sites are better suited for less experienced writers who need to build up their portfolios, recent college graduates, people who need extra income, and experienced freelance writers who need to make a living in between gigs.

If this website or another website on our list alters or updates their posted publishing requirements, submission guidelines or unique payment policies; we will respond by updating this listing as soon as possible. If you have knowledge of any helpful info, please feel free to contact us at hr@writingaxis.com.

#13

Upwork

Overview

The world's largest freelancer marketplace, Upwork resulted from the merger between oDesk and eLance a few years ago.

The platform makes it easy for writers at every skill level to capitalize on the opportunity to work online. Upwork's marketplace is controlled by support vs. demand, and the company has the market cornered so the majority of respectable writing jobs flow this way.

If you'd like to deal with clients privately, Upwork is the place to do it. You'll have to pay a percentage of your earnings to Upwork, but this won't stop you from earning thousands of dollars if you leverage the platform efficiently.

DIGGING DEEPER INTO UPWORK

Upwork can help you find freelance writing jobs; however, it's generally better for building your portfolio or supplementing your income.

You won't get rich with the site, and you will face a number of frustrations.

That said, it is included in this list, because it can offer benefits to inexperienced writers who need to build a portfolio and people who want to make home-based income in their spare time.

Some people love Upwork; some people hate it. In the end, it all depends on your unique situation and your individual expectations.

Get details about writing through Upwork at:

https://writingaxis.com/upwork/

Note: We encourage writers to carefully read through this site's posted publishing requirements, submission guidelines and unique payment policy. Although we always vet each outlet we include in our listings; certain sites are better suited for experienced freelance writers who have impressive portfolios and lots of experience. That said, other sites are better suited for less experienced writers who need to build up their portfolios, recent college graduates, people who need extra income, and experienced freelance writers who need to make a living in between gigs.

If this website or another website on our list alters or updates their posted publishing requirements, submission guidelines or unique payment policies; we will respond by updating this listing as soon as possible. If you have knowledge of any helpful info, please feel free to contact us at hr@writingaxis.com.

#14

Scripted

Overview

Scripted gives writers immediate access to corporate clients who pay up to 10 cents per word.

To gain access, however, you need to get approved as a Scripted writer. This means you will need to be able to show off your talent through writing samples and/or a portfolio.

Since they get contracts from big-name corporations such as eBay, Wal-Mart and Sportchek, scripted is a great place to gain experience and build up your portfolio. When things are busy, you'll see enough work to earn $5,000 or more in a single month.

Since things can slow down, however, you should look to supplement your workflow through another platform or part-time job

DIGGING DEEPER INTO SCRIPTED

Scripted's stated mission is to pair the very best writers with the biggest clients. Scripted writers earn an average of more than ten cents per word and are able to fully control their workload and pricing.

How It Works

Scripted makes it easy and simple for freelance writers to earn good money.

Work Directly with Companies

You can propose jobs directly to clients and build relationships with each one through in-app messaging.

Write in All Sorts of Industries

Scripted new projects every day. Propose jobs to a wide array of project topics.

Payment is Always Guaranteed

With Scripted, you can get paid automatically 15 days after your project is accepted. You can even qualify for partial payments on rejected work.

Make Your Own Prices

Scripted allows you to set your own rates and earn a higher income on requests when you propose the job. Minimum pricing on every job helps to ensure all writers earn a good wage.

Develop a Portfolio

You can host samples of your writing in your Scripted profile. This helps you build out your profile and get clients to come to you.

Set Your Own Schedule

Scripted lets you set your own hours and control your workload. You can take a vacation whenever you want.

Work from Anywhere in the World

With Scripted, you are free to work anywhere with an internet connection. The site currently supports writers in 20-plus countries.

Get details about writing through Scripted at:

https://writingaxis.com/scripted/

Note: We encourage writers to carefully read through this site's posted publishing requirements, submission guidelines and unique payment policy. Although we always vet each outlet we include in our listings; certain sites are better suited for experienced freelance writers who have impressive portfolios and lots of experience. That said, other sites are better suited for less experienced writers who need to build up their portfolios, recent college graduates, people who need extra income, and experienced freelance writers who need to make a living in between gigs.

If this website or another website on our list alters or updates their posted publishing requirements, submission guidelines or unique payment policies; we will respond by updating this listing as soon as possible. If you have knowledge of any helpful info, please feel free to contact us at hr@writingaxis.com.

#15

Zerys

Overview

One of the lesser-known writing platforms, Zerys provides regular work if you check it often.

You will find some amazing earning opportunities if you establish yourself with a quality reputation. You will need to do good work, however, because assignments are handed out based on quality scores from clients.

At Zerys, you can set your own rate, and many top-level clients pay at least 7 cents a word. You can also apply for editing assignments that pay very well if your writing feedback holds strong for a while.

DIGGING DEEPER INTO ZERYS

With the Zerys Writer Network, you can get started for free and there are no bid credits required.

Create a profile, and the platform will notify when a job is posted that matches your skills and interests.

With Zerys, you can develop long-term relationships with customers and build a decently steady source of work.

Bear in mind that Zerys is not an employer but an online content production platform designed to connect freelance writers to companies in search of online content. Zerys is really just a software platform and doesn't employ or contract its users. Writers in the Zerys platform are regarded as self-employed entities, and are called Freelance Service Providers, because they deliver content services to clients who utilize the Zerys platform.

What is the pay rate?

Zerys provides a Direct Assign rate that you want to net out for any direct assignments. It is not going to be actual Client Rate, which will usually be 30% higher than your Direct Assign rate. That extra 30% accounts for Zerys' commission.

If a customer assigns a writing job to you directly, this is the rate they will pay to you, unless they request another rate and you agree to it. You should determine the per-word rate you want based on your experience, availability and experience.

Bear in mind that taken from the board will be only be paid at the specific rate at which it was posted. You won't be paid a Direct Assign rate for these jobs unless the given rate happens to match.

Get details about writing through Zerys at:

https://writingaxis.com/zerys/

Note: We encourage writers to carefully read through this site's posted publishing requirements, submission guidelines and unique payment policy. Although we always vet each outlet we include in our listings; certain sites are better suited for experienced freelance writers who have impressive portfolios and lots of experience. That said, other sites are better suited for less experienced writers who need to build up their portfolios, recent college graduates, people who need extra income, and experienced freelance writers who need to make a living in between gigs.

If this website or another website on our list alters or updates their posted publishing requirements, submission guidelines or unique payment policies; we will respond by updating this listing as soon as possible. If you have knowledge of any helpful info, please feel free to contact us at hr@writingaxis.com.

#16

Content Gather

Overview

Content Gather is a content writing platform that connects writers with website owners who need content (blog posts, articles, press releases, product reviews, product descriptions, how-tos, tutorials and more).

The service gives writers a way to earn money doing what they love and provides website owners with unique, informative content.

Content Gather pays up to 10 cents per word once you have elite status. To gain this status, register on the site, upload a few articles and send an email saying, "please upgrade me."

DIGGING DEEPER INTO CONTENT GATHER

Content Gather provides a platform to connect writers with business owners who need web content, such as articles, blog posts, product descriptions, press releases, product reviews, tutorials, how-tos, and more. In essence, writers get a platform to earn money doing what they like, and business owners get affordable content that helps them sell their products or services.

Fast Payments

With Content Gather, writers can request payment whenever they want and receive money within 24 hours, guaranteed.

Instead of having to wait weeks or months to receive payouts, you can also get paid for pre-written articles. If you are a Silver level writer, you will receive a percentage of your original asking price as soon as you have a pre-written article approved. Then when it sells, you will receive the rest.

Get details about writing for Content Gather at:

https://writingaxis.com/content-gather/

Note: We encourage writers to carefully read through this site's posted publishing requirements, submission guidelines and unique payment policy. Although we always vet each outlet we include in our listings; certain sites are better suited for experienced freelance writers who have impressive portfolios and lots of experience. That said, other sites are better suited for less experienced writers who need to build up their portfolios, recent college graduates, people who need extra income, and experienced freelance writers who need to make a living in between gigs.

If this website or another website on our list alters or updates their posted publishing requirements, submission guidelines or unique payment policies; we will respond by updating this listing as soon as possible. If you have knowledge of any helpful info, please feel free to contact us at hr@writingaxis.com.

#17

iWriter

Or Are You A Writer That Wants To Earn

Overview

iWriter is a good place to supplement your writing work, but it does have its problems.

If you do at least 40 posts without having your quality score drop under 4.85 out of 5, you will be able to see all the higher-paying open Elite Plus jobs. If your score is over 4.6, you can still find a fair number of Elite level assignments on here.

In the end, however, you will probably struggle to make more than $500 a month off iWriter, so try to view it as a way to build your portfolio and/or fill out your workflow.

DIGGING DEEPER INTO IWRITER

iWriter is ones of the easiest, fastest and most reliable ways for businesses to get content written for their websites. Companies post a project on the platform and 1000s of freelance content writers from across the world get instant access to write the content professionally, quickly and affordably.

With iWriter, writers can build a client base and earn up to $80 per 500 words once they get promoted up the ranks. Until then, your pay rate won't be as high.

iWriter accepts writers from North America, Australia, Europe, South America and Asia. They will review your application and email you with a decision within 14 days.

Get details about writing through iWriter at:

https://writingaxis.com/iwriter/

Note: We encourage writers to carefully read through this site's posted publishing requirements, submission guidelines and unique payment policy. Although we always vet each outlet we include in our listings; certain sites are better suited for experienced freelance writers who have impressive portfolios and lots of experience. That said, other sites are better suited for less experienced writers who need to build up their portfolios, recent college graduates, people who need extra income, and experienced freelance writers who need to make a living in between gigs.

If this website or another website on our list alters or updates their posted publishing requirements, submission guidelines or unique payment policies; we will respond by updating this listing as soon as possible. If you have knowledge of any helpful info, please feel free to contact us at hr@writingaxis.com.

#18

HireWriters

Overview

A lower-paying site for less experienced writers, HireWriters is a decent option if you just need to make a few bucks.

Don't expect to break the bank. If you take an assignment, the goal would be to complete it quickly, since most are just basic blog posts for SEO purposes.

If you do it right and type fast, you can make some spare money; however, you should understand that this platform is better suited for younger writers with no experience and those with English language issues who need to build their portfolios and gain some online writing experience.

DIGGING DEEPER INTO IWRITER

If English is your first language, HireWriters.com will give you access to hundreds of low-paid writing jobs. Clients will post writing projects, and you can accept a job and get paid once you completed.

Get paid up to $20 for each article once you become established. Until then, you won't be earning a lot, but you will be able to build your portfolio and get some good experience.

You can work and earn as much as you want, writing about topics of your choosing. You can also get bonus payments from clients whenever you do a good job.

Hire Writers also offers other types of jobs such as: research, proofreading, ideas and, of course, article rewriting.

They pay out every week on Friday, but, again, this outlet isn't designed for experience writers looking to earn big money.

Get details about writing through HireWriters at:

https://writingaxis.com/hire-writers/

Note: We encourage writers to carefully read through this site's posted publishing requirements, submission guidelines and unique payment policy. Although we always vet each outlet we include in our listings; certain sites are better suited for experienced freelance writers who have impressive portfolios and lots of experience. That said, other sites are better suited for less experienced writers who need to build up their portfolios, recent college graduates, people who need extra income, and experienced freelance writers who need to make a living in between gigs.

If this website or another website on our list alters or updates their posted publishing requirements, submission guidelines or unique payment policies; we will respond by updating this listing as soon as possible. If you have knowledge of any helpful info, please feel free to contact us at hr@writingaxis.com.

#19

CopyPress

Overview

CopyPress is a unique writing platform that doesn't function like the traditional writer's mill.

Instead of merely throwing work in front of writers, CopyPress scouts for great writing talent and matches people to contracts.

In addition to functioning as a paid writing site, CopyPress is a network where writers can interact. There are many writers who have been matched with corporate clients and now earn $20 to $60 an hour, all thanks to their free CopyPress membership.

DIGGING DEEPER INTO COPYPRESS

What We Do

Creating things is a unifying passion at CopyPress. Since 2009, we've fed that passion by building software, products, and services that help creatives and advertisers do the same.

We built a Community where writers, designers, and developers can create their own micro-businesses centered around their passion. CopyPress and our proprietary software is the conduit for this community and our clients to create engaging campaigns with compelling content.

Our ability to connect our large community of trained creatives with clients ranging from mid-market companies to digital agencies and Fortune 500 organizations allows us to do what we love: build tools that enable both creatives and advertisers to scale, promote, and most importantly, create.

Contact CopyPress and request a screening invitation.

https://writingaxis.com/copy-press/

Note: We encourage writers to carefully read through this site's posted publishing requirements, submission guidelines and unique payment policy. Although we always vet each outlet we include in our listings; certain sites are better suited for experienced freelance writers who have impressive portfolios and lots of experience. That said, other sites are better suited for less experienced writers who need to build up their portfolios, recent college graduates, people who need extra income, and experienced freelance writers who need to make a living in between gigs.

If this website or another website on our list alters or updates their posted publishing requirements, submission guidelines or unique payment policies; we will respond by updating this listing as soon as possible. If you have knowledge of any helpful info, please feel free to contact us at hr@writingaxis.com.

#20

Crowd Content

Overview

Crowd Content is a scalable content marketplace for agencies, brands and retailers.

From a writer's point of view, the platform offers a very diverse pay scale, which runs from a few cents per word up to $1.75 per word.

If you accept a lot of jobs and these jobs are reviewed positively, you will be matched with higher paying gigs.

DIGGING DEEPER INTO CROWD CONTENT

With Crowd Content, you can access content writing jobs, claim orders and write content for a diverse collection of clients.

You will notice quickly that this platform is a bit different from other writing companies. This is because they've added a little gamification into the mix.

What's gamification? It's essentially the use of game mechanics and game-thinking in non-game contexts solve problems and to engage users. Gamification is used in processes and applications to improve ROI, user engagement, data quality, learning and timeliness.

In other words, Crowd Content tracks a variety of key performance metrics for each writer in its system. Writers who perform well and tally good stats are rewarded; those who don't are note.

When you sign into your account, click on your profile picture in the top right corner. There you can view your current performance levels.

Get details about writing for Crowd Content at:

https://writingaxis.com/crowd-content/

Note: We encourage writers to carefully read through this site's posted publishing requirements, submission guidelines and unique payment policy. Although we always vet each outlet we include in our listings; certain sites are better suited for experienced freelance writers who have impressive portfolios and lots of experience. That said, other sites are better suited for less experienced writers who need to build up their portfolios, recent college graduates, people who need extra income, and experienced freelance writers who need to make a living in between gigs.

If this website or another website on our list alters or updates their posted publishing requirements, submission guidelines or unique payment policies; we will respond by updating this listing as soon as possible. If you have knowledge of any helpful info, please feel free to contact us at hr@writingaxis.com.

#21

TextBroker

Overview

Since 2005, Textbroker has been one of the leading providers of unique, custom content.

It's one of the very first content mills, and it hasn't changed a whole lot over time. If you are just starting out, Textbroker gives you access to thousands of diverse writing opportunities for a wide array of topics. You can choose when and how much content you write, and there is no limit to how much you can earn.

Unfortunately, TextBroker doesn't pay very well until you level up by writing a specified amount of well-received content. Even then, you won't be making much more than 5 cents per word. Still, it's a good place to get experience or make some extra money if you don't have a very substantial writing portfolio.

DIGGING DEEPER INTO TEXTBROKER

With Textbroker, you can earn money writing content; however, you won't get paid a great rate.

Since 2005, Textbroker has been a leading provider of custom written content. Thousands of registered customers and authors from all over the world execute more than 150,000 content orders through the platform every month. Its clients include small business owners, publicly traded corporations, e-commerce websites, publishing houses and social media communities.

If you are just starting out as a writer, Textbroker gives you access to countless writing opportunities for a variety of topics. Decide when and how much content you write; there's no limit; however, again, you shouldn't expect to get rich with this site.

Why Should You Write for Textbroker?

The platform offers reliable payment and flexible time management. It also allows you to build up a portfolio and gain some experience that will allow you to secure higher-paying gigs down the line. In short, Textbroker is a writer's mill where you can pay your dues and refine your writing skills while earning some extra cash at the same time.

Get details about writing for Textbroker at:

https://writingaxis.com/text-broker/

Note: We encourage writers to carefully read through this site's posted publishing requirements, submission guidelines and unique payment policy. Although we always vet each outlet we include in our listings; certain sites are better suited for experienced freelance writers who have impressive portfolios and lots of experience. That said, other sites are better suited for less experienced writers who need to build up their portfolios, recent college graduates, people who need extra income, and experienced freelance writers who need to make a living in between gigs.

If this website or another website on our list alters or updates their posted publishing requirements, submission guidelines or unique payment policies; we will respond by updating this listing as soon as possible. If you have knowledge of any helpful info, please feel free to contact us at hr@writingaxis.com.

#22

The Content Authority

Overview

The Content Authority is another content writing platform that connects writers with website owners who need blog posts, articles, press releases, product reviews, product descriptions, etc.

Pay varies, with the lowest starting at less than one cent per word and the highest at 3 cents per word. Once you hit $25 in your account, you can cash in and get paid via PayPal.

This is another place you should only choose if you need experience, have trouble with English, just want to make a few extra dollars or don't have a very substantial writing portfolio.

DIGGING DEEPER INTO THE CONTENT AUTHORITY

The Content Authority is another good place for inexperienced freelance writers who want to build up a portfolio and get some much-needed experience. It's also a good place to monetize your writing skills if you need to earn a little extra money as a side gig.

The Content Authority's primary goal is to supply web entrepreneurs and existing businesses with relevant content that will engage customers and add value to their websites. With a focus on providing quality for less money, the platform's objective is to give businesses the edge they need to compete with bigger competitors and succeed in highly competitive markets.

To write for The Content Authority you will need to satisfy some minimal requirements:

- You must be able to read, write and comprehend English.
- You must be able use proper English grammar to write formal articles at a high school level.
- You must have the ability to do good research about an array of topics based on the requirements of the company's clients.
- You must be able to follow the guidelines of clients and adhere to the requirements of The Content Authority.
- You must be able and willing to write content within strict deadlines.
- You must be able to be paid via PayPal.
- You must be willing to accept critiques from both clients and editors.

Get details about writing for The Content Authority at:

https://writingaxis.com/the-content-authority/

Note: We encourage writers to carefully read through this site's posted publishing requirements, submission guidelines and unique payment policy. Although we always vet each outlet we include in our listings; certain sites are better suited for experienced freelance writers who have impressive portfolios and lots of experience. That said, other sites are better suited for less experienced writers who need to build up their portfolios, recent college graduates, people who need extra income, and experienced freelance writers who need to make a living in between gigs.

If this website or another website on our list alters or updates their posted publishing requirements, submission guidelines or unique payment policies; we will respond by updating this listing as soon as possible. If you have knowledge of any helpful info, please feel free to contact us at hr@writingaxis.com.

#23

Listverse

Overview

Listverse will pay for interesting list articles about anything, as long as the topic is unusual, unique or interesting.

The site will pay you $100 for every approved list, and the editors generally want articles to be around 1,500 words and feature at least 10 items.

If you have a Twitter account, blog or a novel you would like to promote, mention it in the site's submissions form, and Listverse will promote it at the bottom of your list.

DIGGING DEEPER INTO LISTVERSE

Listverse was built by readers who did not have much experience as writers, but it would be fun to start putting lists together and publish them on the web. Since that time, it's grown into one of the most popular sites on the internet.

They will pay you $100 for any great lists they approve. You won't need to be an expert on a given topic; — you simply need to be a native English speaker (or be able to fake it) who has a sense of humor and a love for interesting and unusual things.

With Listverse, you write up a list (10 items minimum) and send it in. If they like it, they'll publish it and send you $100 by PayPal. If they don't like it, they will let you know and ask you to send in something else if they like your writing or thought process. Just remember, every list needs to be at least one or two paragraphs.

If it's approved, your list will appear on the front page of Listverse and get read by millions of people.

Listverse won't accept lists from anyone without a PayPal account. If PayPal doesn't support your country, don't bother requesting alternative methods of payment.

Get details about writing for Listverse at:

https://writingaxis.com/listverse/

Note: We encourage writers to carefully read through this site's posted publishing requirements, submission guidelines and unique payment policy. Although we always vet each outlet we include in our listings; certain sites are better suited for experienced freelance writers who have impressive portfolios and lots of experience. That said, other sites are better suited for less experienced writers who need to build up their portfolios, recent college graduates, people who need extra income, and experienced freelance writers who need to make a living in between gigs.

If this website or another website on our list alters or updates their posted publishing requirements, submission guidelines or unique payment policies; we will respond by updating this listing as soon as possible. If you have knowledge of any helpful info, please feel free to contact us at hr@writingaxis.com.

#24

Sitepoint

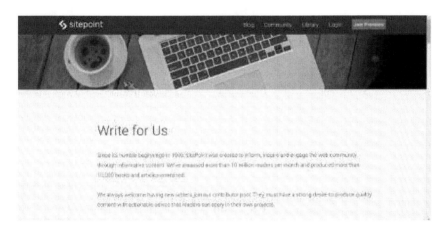

Overview

Sitepoint pays for content that is instructive, technical, well-written and innovative.

Sitepoint writers are typically web professionals with a passion for design and development. The site has amassed more than 10 million readers per month and produced more than 10,000 articles and books.

They are always looking for new writers to join their contributor pool. Pay varies, but you can expect to make above-industry rates for quality articles about CSS, JavaScript, PHP, Ruby, Mobile development, UX, Design and HTML.

DIGGING DEEPER INTO SITEPOINT

Sitepoint is always looking for new writers join its contributor pool. Bear in mind, you will need to be able to produce quality content that contains actionable advice readers can use in their own projects

In return, Sitepoint will pay you above-industry rates for your work.

What kind of content does Sitepoint publish?

Every month, Sitepoint produces a hub that focus its energies on a single technical topic, creating content across books and articles that provide readers with a clear, linear path to competency in that specific skill. In recent months, the site has created hubs covering web performance, analytics and other technical topics.

In future months, it will be looking at subjects like Angular, Vue, Node and UX prototyping. Sitepoint adds to its list of planned hubs every quarter.

In general, the content required for every hub is determined by the hub editor and assigned to any available writers with experience in that topic. Sitepoint welcome's ideas from writers when hubs are in their planning phases; however, pitching specific article ideas is not typically a part of our editorial process.

In short: you can make really good money at Sitepoint, but your will need a technical background.

Get details about writing for Sitepoint at:

https://writingaxis.com/sitepoint/

Note: We encourage writers to carefully read through this site's posted publishing requirements, submission guidelines and unique payment policy. Although we always vet each outlet we include in our listings; certain sites are better suited for experienced freelance writers who have impressive portfolios and lots of experience. That said, other sites are better suited for less experienced writers who need to build up their portfolios, recent college graduates, people who need extra income, and experienced freelance writers who need to make a living in between gigs.

If this website or another website on our list alters or updates their posted publishing requirements, submission guidelines or unique payment policies; we will respond by updating this listing as soon as possible. If you have knowledge of any helpful info, please feel free to contact us at hr@writingaxis.com.

#25

Online Writing Jobs

Overview

Formerly known as QualityGal, Online Writing Jobs has been paying writers for content since 2006.

The platform uses a rubric-driven, per-project pay scale, and final payment relates to the specific grade indicated by the rubric.

With that said, average payout ranges from $10 to $27 per project, based on the project specs.

DIGGING DEEPER INTO ONLINE WRITING JOBS

Previously known as QualityGal, Online Writing Jobs has been around for nearly 20 years. The site was renamed because it has grown surprisingly popular and a more relevant domain name became available.

It is limited to United States-based writers who can show the required documentation.

It uses a rubric-driven, per-project pay scale, and final payment depends on the grade indicated by the rubric. Average payouts tend to fall between $10 and $27 and per project, depending on the individual project specs.

Writers can invoice whenever they want, and Online Writing Jobs will pay weekly via check or PayPal.

You can also showcase your niche knowledge and writing skills with additional dedicated, direct-offer writing opportunities.

Get details about writing for Online Writing Jobs at:

https://writingaxis.com/online-writing-jobs/

Note: We encourage writers to carefully read through this site's posted publishing requirements, submission guidelines and unique payment policy. Although we always vet each outlet we include in our listings; certain sites are better suited for experienced freelance writers who have impressive portfolios and lots of experience. That said, other sites are better suited for less experienced writers who need to build up their portfolios, recent college graduates, people who need extra income, and experienced freelance writers who need to make a living in between gigs.

If this website or another website on our list alters or updates their posted publishing requirements, submission guidelines or unique payment policies; we will respond by updating this listing as soon as possible. If you have knowledge of any helpful info, please feel free to contact us at hr@writingaxis.com.

WHERE TO FIND HIGHER PAYING WRITING JOBS

If you talk to most successful freelance writers, chances are, they have used a job board to land higher-paying gigs.

It's important to understand that, while job boards are a premier source for freelance writing jobs, the competition can be tough. You will be going against writers with lots of experience and impressive portfolios.

Still, while it can get intense, job boards definitely offer high rewards as long as you are willing to put in the effort.

Here are a few of our favorites:

#*1*

Journalism Jobs

Overview

This is a great place where experienced writers can find higher paying jobs from some of the world's biggest brands, including ESPN, Slate.com, Time Magazine, National Geographic Magazine, C-Span, USA Today, CNN, Fox News Channel, Wall Street Journal, HuffingtonPost.com, PBS, MSNBC, Newsweek, New York Times, Boston Globe, Reuters, Financial Times, Los Angeles Times, Atlanta Journal-Constitution, Dow Jones, Bloomberg, NPR, Associated Press, Forbes Magazine, Business Week, Fortune, America Online, Fast Company, Men's Health, Wired, Mother Jones, U.S. News & World Report, Cosmopolitan, Reader's Digest, Discovery Channel, ABCNews.com, TheStreet.com, Boston Herald, New York Post, San Francisco Chronicle, trade associations, PR agencies, journalism schools and noteworthy newsletter groups.

Get more details here:

https://writingaxis.com/journalism-jobs/

#2
Media Bistro

Overview

Mediabistro offers resources and employment opportunities for experienced writers and media professionals. It in addition to its classifieds section, the site publishes various blogs which look into the entire mass media industry, including publishing and film industries. It also provides seminars, courses and, of course, job listings.

At Mediabistro, you can browse hundreds of jobs from the largest media companies. You can also get advice, learn new skills, access tools. And connect with hiring managers to elevate your freelance career.

Get more details here:

https://writingaxis.com/media-bistro/

#3
People Per Hour

Overview

Cloud-based platforms have made it much easier for digital agencies to find talented writers from a global talent pool. It has also made it easier for freelancers to market their skills.

PeoplePerHour is an internet community of freelance professionals that helps businesses outsource projects to skilled remote workers.

Get more details here:

https://writingaxis.com/people-per-hour/

#4

Freelance Writing Gigs

Overview

Owned by Splashpress Media, this great website has developed into one of the leading destinations for freelance writers. It's a great place where freelance writers can grow, learn, discuss issues and ask questions.

Perhaps most importantly, however, the site posts new freelance writing and blogging jobs every day. Whether you're a beginner or seasoned writer, the information you need to be successful is readily available at Freelance Writing Jobs.

Get more details here:

https://writingaxis.com/freelance-writing-gigs/

#5
All of Craigslist

Overview

Craigslist continues to be one of the leading ways professional writers find high-paying jobs online. Unfortunately, it can be difficult to view every available opportunity, without visiting the CL page for every single major city.

This invaluable resource allows you to search all of Craigslist in a matter of minutes. Easily search for writing jobs by typing common keywords, such as "content writer," "freelance writing," and more.

Get more details here:

https://writingaxis.com/all-of-craigslist/

#6
Linked In

Overview

If you're looking for a high-paying writing job in your city or lucrative remote writing work, LinkedIn is a great place to start.

Most major companies leverage this platform when looking for writing talent. You can also post your resume and portfolio so companies can find you.

Get more details here:

https://writingaxis.com/linkedin/

#7
Zeerk

Overview

Zeerk allows writers and other freelance professionals to secure micro jobs that pay from $3 to $200.

Jobs include:

- Articles and Blog Posts
- Creative Writing
- Business Names and Taglines
- Product Descriptions
- Proofreading & Editing
- Translation
- Press Releases
- Transcripts
- Resumes and Cover Letters
- eBook Services
- Web

Get more details here:

https://writingaxis.com/zeerk/

#8
Indeed

Overview

The world's #1 job site, Indeed gives you free access to post resumes, search for jobs and research companies. Much like Craigslist, it's one of the best ways for writers to find remote freelance work and high-paying writing jobs in their cities.

Easily search for jobs by typing common keywords, such as "content writer," "freelance writer," and more. It's generally best to sort each search by date to make sure your application gets near the front of the line.

Get more details here:

https://writingaxis.com/indeed/

#9
Blogging Pro Job Board

Overview

This resource is updated daily with new paid blog writing jobs, blogging jobs and freelance writing gigs.

For freelance writers and bloggers, they do the job searching. For businesses and individuals in need of high-quality content, they open the door to reliable talent. Check the site daily if you're looking for writing work that pays higher rates per piece.

Get more details here:

https://writingaxis.com/blogging-pro-job-board/

#10
Morning Coffee eNewsletter

Receive automatic job alerts of new freelance writing jobs every morning.

Since 1956, FreelanceWriting.com has been publishing the "Morning Coffee" eNewsletter featuring new and updated freelance writing jobs. The weekly digest contains 8 of the best new writing jobs for freelancers. We feature jobs submitted exclusively to FreelanceWriting.com. We also research and handpick jobs from popular job sites like Indeed, Craigslist, Problogger, and others. You can also find these jobs updated 24/7 in our ONLINE ACTION JOB STORE — including special writing gigs submitted to FreelanceWriting.com exclusively.

Overview

Provided by FreelanceWriting.com, this newsletter is an excellent resource for writers in search of freelance blogging work. The weekly email comes with brief descriptions of each opportunity, so you only need to click on the links that make sense for you.

Sign up to receive updates if you're looking for regular writing work.

Get more details here:

https://writingaxis.com/morning-coffee-enewsletter/

35 *More*
Websites that
Will Pay You to Write

Download from Amazon here

"A really great resource for writers in search of good pay for home-based work."
— *KingofHowTo.com Book Reviews*

In this sequel to "25 Websites that Will Pay You to Write," you will find 35 additional websites that will pay you to write articles, blog posts, product descriptions and more.

Get even more. Thirty-five extra sites that will pay you up to $1,500 per article.
New to writing? An experienced pro? This honest, informative book will help you take the next step in you work-from-home writing career.

Includes:

- 35 websites that provide regular work for writers
- Sites that pay up to **$1,500 per article**, $70 per hour and $1.75 per word
- In-depth overviews providing insight into each opportunity
- Links to the websites, so you can easily apply

Download from Amazon here

(Free for Kindle Unlimited subscribers.)

ADDITIONAL WRITING RESOURCES

If you're looking for some great insight and guidance to help kickstart a new writing career or take your existing career to the next level, the following resources are highly recommended.

1) How to Make a Living as a Writer
by James Scott Bell

RESOURCE OVERVIEW

It's the very best time on Earth to be a freelance writer

More writers are earning money today than at any other period in history. For centuries, very few have been able to really support themselves from the keyboard or quill alone.

No longer. With the rise of indie publishing and eBooks, there are now more chances than ever for writers to make substantial money from their written work. And there is still an ever-growing traditional publishing industry that requires new talent to keep on growing.

In this book, you will learn the secrets of how to write for profit and increase your chances of making a good wage from your written work. Here are some of the topics covered:

- The Secrets of Today's Writing Success
- How to Identify and Reach Your Goals
- The Essentials of Your Individual Writing Business
- Keys to a REAL Winning System
- Unlocking Your Unique Creativity
- How to Always Stay Relentless
- How to Write Faster
- Going Traditional
- Comparing Self- and Traditional Publishing
- Going Indie
- How to Craft a Novel in one Month
- How to Form Numerous Streams of Written Income
- How to Maintain a Positive Mental Outlook
- How to Find Great Non-Fiction Subjects
- Resources for More Study

Learn how to earn what you're worth and write what you love.

Get this resource here:

https://www.amazon.com/dp/B00P1JGD8I/

2) *Writer's Market 2019*
The Most Trusted Guide to Getting Published
by Robert Lee Brewer

RESOURCE OVERVIEW

Would you like to get published and make money for your writing? Let the Writer's Market 2019 help you learn the process with countless publishing opportunities, including listings for consumer and trade magazines, book publishers, literary agents and contests and awards, along with new screenwriting and playwriting sections.

These listings include submission and contact information to help you get your work published.

Beyond these numerous listings, you will also find all-new material devoted to the promotion and business of writing. Learn how to profit covering live events and find out the secrets to ten-minute marketing. Plus, you will find out how to do create a business plan, video more effectively and much, much more. This edition also includes the popular book publisher subject index and pay-rate chart.

You also acquire access to:

- Several sample query letters
- Lists of pro writing organizations
- A complimentary digital download of Writer's YB, featuring the very Best Markets

Also includes exclusive access to Robert Lee Brewer's webinar "Find More Success with Your Submissions."

Get this resource here:

https://www.amazon.com/dp/B07GRHFD5 6/

3) *Make Money Writing on the STEEM Blockchain*

A Short Beginner's Guide to Earning Cryptocurrency Online, Through Blogging on Steemit (Convert to Bitcoin, U.S. Dollars, and Other Currencies)

by James Scott Bell

Overview

The blockchain has revolutionized how professional writers get paid. This brief guide will help you become a viable part of it.

Learn how to turn the STEEM you make into real spendable cash.

Find out how to increase your earnings by selecting the correct tags and managing your STEEM intelligently.

Get your writing seen by more people and make money for every single upvote your posts earn.

Get this resource here:

https://www.amazon.com/dp/B07CYJM1JB/

4) *Kindle Bestseller Publishing (2019)*
Publish a #1 Bestseller in the next 30 Days!
by Gundi Gabrielle

RESOURCE OVERVIEW

Learn how to write and publish an Amazon eBook bestseller in 30 Days.

With proper research and the right strategy, it is very possible, even if:

- You aren't a writer
- You don't yet have a big following
- You don't have marketing experience

As a 12-time bestselling author, Gundi Gabrielle knows a lot about writing and publishing bestseller books.

Every one of her eBooks has reached number one within a few days of publishing and she has developed a proven, easy-to-follow system that has helped numerous first-time writers around the world reach best-seller status within weeks. They even beat out famous authors such as Hal Elrod, Tim Ferriss, Brian Tracy and John Grisham and Brian Tracy.

This book is part of the SassyZenGirl INFLUENCER series, designed to teach digital marketing to beginners. You may not think of Amazon Publishing as an effective marketing tool, but it is actually:

One of the quickest, most efficient strategies for building a following online.

For your social media platforms, your blog, your company or any other service you offer.

Publishing on Amazon also offers the following advantages:

- Instant credibility in your given field
- New customers and clients on autopilot who will trust you, because you have proven yourself

- The status of being a published - or even top-selling - author
- Passive income and automated list building. Email marketing is considered the top marketing technique, more than Google Ads and Facebook combined. By publishing your eBook on Amazon, you can build your mailing list and Amazon will even pay you to do it.

This book teaches you how to go from zero to a published top-seller.

This book focuses on the Marketing angle of publishing on Amazon and teaches you what it takes to reach top-seller status.

Important topics include:

- Researching how to come up with profitable book ideas
- Keyword and Category Research and how top seller ranking on Amazon works
- How to create optimized meta data, including your title to trigger algorithmic activity to promote your book better
- Understanding Amazon's unique algorithm and how new visitors can find you
- How to market your new eBook during the all-important Launch Weekend

Get this resource here:

https://www.amazon.com/dp/B06XKGGW RC/

5) *Lifelong Writing Habit*
The Secret to Writing Every Day
Write Faster, Write Smarter
by Chris Fox

RESOURCE OVERVIEW

Are you sick of writing intermittently if at all? Wouldn't you like to create a lifelong writing routine that gets your ass in the chair every day? If so, this is the book for you. This book draws on proven neuroscience techniques to help you cultivate a daily writing routine that will last the rest of your life.

It provides an easy-to-understand strategy with actionable steps at the conclusion of each chapter.

In this book, you will learn:

- How to create a permanent life-long writing habit
- How to get more organized
- How to develop and achieve impressive writing goals
- How to harness motivation and self-discipline

Make a permanent shift in your writing habits and achieve your highest goals.

Get this resource here:

https://www.amazon.com/dp/B014V7PXV8/

6) *The Workplace Writer's Process*
A Guide to Getting the Job Done

by Anne Janzer

RESOURCE OVERVIEW

If writing is any place in your current job, you really need to figure out how to get it done efficiently, consistently and successfully.

In this eBook, you will learn business communication skills they don't go over in a typical writing class:

Find out how to streamline collaboration with subject matter experts and stakeholders
Discover the most efficient way to approach necessary revisions
Learn to embrace the style guide as a friend, and discover how to make one for your company
Find out how to set up every project to sail through approvals and reviews

This book is filled with all sorts of actionable tips you can use right away to create content and complete more projects in less time. Get it today to invest in your success.

Get this resource here:

https://www.amazon.com/dp/B073K8XTHC/

7) Writer's Digest Guide to Magazine Article Writing

A Practical Guide to Selling Your Pitches, Crafting Strong Articles, & Earning More Bylines

by Kerrie Flanagan, Angela Mackintosh

RESOURCE OVERVIEW

This is the essential reference for writing content for magazines.

In this book, accomplished freelance author, writer and instructor, Kerrie Flanagan, rejects the idea that writing for magazines is a hard process meant only for people with degrees in journalism.

Drawing from her two decades of a freelance instructor and writer, the author takes you through the whole process, step-by-step, sharing her experiences and knowledge in a conversational, friendly manner.

With expert advice from editors, more than twelve sample articles and tips from successful writers, this book includes instructions on making compelling query letters along with practical tips on researching publications.

In this book you will learn how to:

• Negotiate and checklists contracts.
• Target and discover ideas for each magazine.
• Organize your writing life using the tools and checklists throughout the eBook.
• Develop impactful query letters to snare the attention of head editors and get more assignments.
• Sell and write personal essays to niche consumer and trade magazines.

Whether you are trying to get your first byline or become a full-time freelance writer; this book is your go-to source for writing success.

Get this resource here:

https://www.amazon.com/dp/B07GRKQBS L/

8) *Become a Writer Today*
by Bryan Collins

RESOURCE OVERVIEW

Would you like to get paid to write?

Or maybe you would like to self-publish an eBook or become a successful fiction or nonfiction author.

It can be scary taking your writing more seriously and becoming a published author unless you have a little help.

Now, with this series, you can get three books that will help you excel all kinds of writing for one affordable price.

(Book 1)
Many new writers say they can't handle about writer's block. It's time to overcome that problem.

In this practical resource, the author has gathered 101 of the top writing prompts. Use them for fiction, nonfiction, journal writing, blogging and your next book.

The basic truth is you can write virtually anything with the right prompt.

(Book 2)
Are you a slow to moderately slow writer?

Learn proven productivity tactics top authors and writers use to succeed. Find out how to get the words out and finish your book or stories much faster.

(Book 3)
Who says you can't earn good money by writing? Almost everybody has some type of idea for a book; but just a few of them turn their ideas into a money-making reality.

In this book, the author explains what need to know about publishing, writing and selling a top-selling non-fiction book.

Get this resource here:

https://www.amazon.com/dp/B07CR51CX N/

9) *The Five-Day Novel*
The How to Guide for Writing Faster & Optimizing Your Workflow

by Scott King

RESOURCE OVERVIEW

Have trouble finishing your novels?

Elevate your workflow process and write your book in just five days.

After taking far too long to finish a fantasy epic, educator and author Scott King tweaked his writing process and learned how to start and complete a novel in only five days.

With helpful examples and easy-to-follow tips, the author takes a theme and crafts a full story around it. Let him show you the pre-writing process, how to get through the first draft and do rewrites in a timely manner.

In this book, you will find out:

- How to develop the right mindset
- How to eliminate distractions and better manage your time
- Learn the ingredients needed to form a great story
- How to keep focus and continue writing every day
- How to better plan each of your rewrites
- Learn what to look for when line editing

If you want an honest, no bull, book with a little humor and many of examples, you will love this behind-the-scenes look at writing a novel in only five days.

Get this resource here:

https://www.amazon.com/dp/B01MDN3015/

10) *The Writer's Process*
Getting Your Brain in Gear

by Anne Janzer

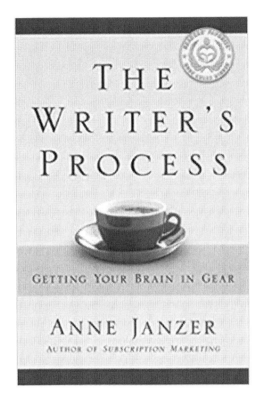

RESOURCE OVERVIEW

Want to learn how to be a much better writer? You need to improve your process.

Are you afraid of the blank page? You might be skipping the critical early phases of the writing process.

Do you come up with tons of ideas but never seem to publish anything? You need tactics to focus and keep going right to the finish.

When you learn how to work in concert with your brain instead of constantly working against it, you will get a lot more done and have a lot more fun.

This book combines cognitive science research with proven practices of successful writers to teach you:

- How to invite flow and creativity into the writing process
- How you can become more productive by separating your writing into different steps
- How to sidestep writer's block, overcome negative feedback, and ditch distractions
- How to make more time for writing in the midst of your busy life

Get this resource here:

https://www.amazon.com/dp/B01G99B5LS
/

11) *Stop Worrying; Start Writing*
How to Overcome Fear, Self-Doubt and Procrastination

by Sarah Painter

RESOURCE OVERVIEW

Do you have a great desire to write but cannot get started? Are you having trouble finishing your novel or frustrated by your delayed progress? Maybe you are beginning to worry you are not cut out to be a writer at all.

Let top-selling novelist and podcast host, Sarah Painter teach your how to free-up writing time, ditch negativity, beat procrastination and cope with self-doubt.

With insight from top authors such as Julie Cohen, Mark Edwards and C.L.Taylor, Mark Edwards, this book will show:

- How to get past writing blocks to complete stories faster
- How to avoid self-doubt that keeps you from creating
- How to trick your mind into becoming more productive
- Hoe to plan your time to maximize your productivity and satisfaction

Plus, many more tricks and tips!

Packed with supportive, honest and hard-won tips, this is your go-to guide to getting more work done.

Why let creative anxiety put an end to your writing dreams? Quit worrying and begin the writing journey.

Get this resource here:

https://www.amazon.com/dp/B06Y6GXFY6/

12) Declutter Your Mind
How to Stop Worrying, Relieve Anxiety, and Eliminate Negative Thinking

by S.J. Scott & Barrie Davenport

RESOURCE OVERVIEW

Are you overwhelmed by thoughts? Do you struggle with anxiety about your everyday tasks? Would you like to quit worrying about life?

We all have negative thoughts from time to time. If you always seem to feel overwhelmed, however, you need to assess how these thoughts could be negatively impacting your life.

The solution? To practice proven mindfulness techniques that allow your mind to enjoy happiness and inner peace. With these daily habits, you will have the space and clarity to prioritize the most important things in your life. You will also learn to let go of what no longer serves you and decide how you want to live life on a daily basis.

The goal of this eBook is simple: The author wants to teach you the actions, habits and mindsets to clear the mental clutter that might be keeping you from living a meaningful life.

You will learn:

- How to reframe negative thoughts
- The primary causes of mental clutter
- The importance of ditching the distractions that lead to anxiety
- Ways to improve or end bad relationships
- A simple way to discover what is really important to you
- Words that will help you identify YOUR distinctive values
- The advantages of focused deep breathing and meditation
- How to develop goals that connect you to your passions

This book is filled with exercises that will have a positive, immediate effect on your mindset. Instead of just telling you why you should do something; the author provides science-backed, practical actions that can create lasting change when regularly practiced.

Get this resource here:

https://www.amazon.com/dp/B01KU04K5A/

13) *Make A REAL LIVING as a Freelance Writer*
How to Win Top Writing Assignments

by Jenna Glatzer

RESOURCE OVERVIEW

This book contains helpful instructions on how freelance writers can make money writing for magazines.

It reveals secrets about:

- What high-paying magazines really look for
- How to determine which sections of magazines are open to freelance writers
- How to become an experienced expert in your chosen writing field
- How to cultivate relationships with editors
- What types of stories are in highest demand
- How to market your reprints
- What to do if a publisher won't pay up

The book defines key terms, such as clips, query and source sheet, while providing tips on everything from generating ideas to pitching syndicated columns. Writers can also learn about the lesser-known sources top freelance writers use to discover new stories. Writers can also learn how to:

- Get their very first paying projects even if they have no prior samples
- Negotiate for better pay
- Find higher-paying magazines that aren't overwhelmed with queries
- Get into editors' inboxes even without publicized e-mail

Get this resource here:

https://www.amazon.com/dp/B00CNVOH26/

14) *Activate Your Brain*
How Understanding Your Brain Can Improve Your Work - and Your Life

by Scott G. Halford

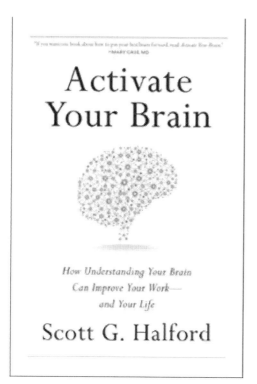

RESOURCE OVERVIEW

Learn how to push your brain to its full potential for success at home and at the office.

Do you want more control over your work and life?

Would you like to develop increased stamina to help you carry out your everyday tasks?

How about learning how to get more meaning and significance in your career?

In this book, the author shows you how to find these things by activating the full potential of your brain. This amazing organ is still filled with mystery; however, we know enough to leverage its power better than ever before. You simply need to recognize how your brain thinks and understand the steps you can take to help it perform better.

Combining anecdotes, research and inspiration, the book shows you how minor steps toward better brain management and function can lead to success in every facet of your life.

Every chapter offers activation exercises that help optimize brain function to:

Enhance your focus
Eliminate negative stress
Build willpower and self-confidence
Collaborate better with others
Ditch distractions

Discover an indispensable collection of practical information about your incredible brain, which, when fully empowered, can help you achieve a more fulfilled life.

Get this resource here:

https://www.amazon.com/dp/B00WUNSFC
A/

15) *Six Figure Blogging Blueprint*
How to Start an Amazingly Profitable Blog in the Next 60 Days (Even If You Have No Experience)

by Raza Imam

RESOURCE OVERVIEW

Find out how to start a profitable blog in the next two months even if you don't have experience.

Looking for a reliable step-by-step strategy that will help you earn a profit by putting your blog on autopilot?

Ready to make income blogging, but don't know how to start?

Imagine what it would be like if you could see regular blog money funneling into your bank account.

Once you master this simple process, you will be able to work from any place in the world.

You will be able to quit your dead-end job for good.

And you will be able to create a passive income business and earn profits every single day.

In this short but impactful book, the author reveals his story of creating a profitable passive income blogging business.

You will learn how to do it too, step by step.

The author shows you how to get similar results as other supper-successful bloggers. Even if you have a steady full-time job.

In this informative book, you will learn:

- The most popular topics to write about
- The effective content strategy to attract countless eager readers
- Getting set up the simple, fast way (web hosting, content management system and domain names

- How to make great blog posts that will go viral and create massive traffic
- The secrets of to making a responsive, beautiful blog easily and quickly
- The powerful secret to building rapport with an audience

And much more

Stop gambling with your hard-won money.

Join the many of intelligent professionals that have leveraged their expertise to make regular passive income from home using their blogs.

Get this resource here:

https://www.amazon.com/dp/B07R7Z2H69

16) Blogging: Getting To $2,000 A Month

by Isaac Kronenberg

RESOURCE OVERVIEW

This informative book is one of the most advanced blogging resources on the market, teaching the most effective monetization strategies to get your weblog from nothing to thousands of dollars a month in just ninety days.

All the content in this resource is based on real, effective tactics used by the top-earning bloggers on the web. Whether you are new to blogging or an experienced blogger, this book is the closest thing to a magic pill that can take you from absolutely nothing to making a full-time income just from your blog.

If you are dead serious about making money blogging, this resource is one of the best books you can read on the subject.

Get this resource here:

https://www.amazon.com/dp/B072FHKFFG/

17) Ten Quick Wins for Writers
How to ignite creativity, write steadily, and publish your book

by Jed Jurchenko

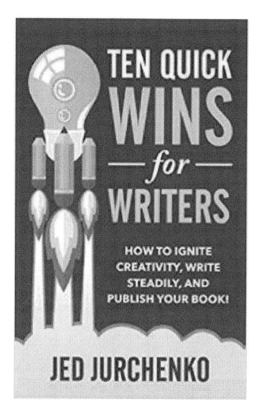

RESOURCE OVERVIEW

Write with ease, spark creativity and grow your daily writing habit. This motivation resource is packed with all sorts of powerful writing tools to help guide you on the journey.

While countless people wish they could publish, only a small few actually achieve this goal.

Common barriers include:

- Fear of failure
- Writer's block
- Concerns that publishing will be hard
- Inconsistent daily writing habits
- Confusion about how to proceed

Fear of being rejected

These ten writing tools will help you craft content steadily and discover:

- A pair of words that change everything
- The secret to completing your book
- How to enjoy writing
- How to write better, faster
- Defeat writer's block
- How to develop persistence
- A powerful motivation metaphor
- How to develop laser focus

For years, the author wanted to finish writing a book. Unfortunately, he fell into the usual pattern of starting well only to get sidetracked and ultimately quit. Then, he discovered effective writing tools that changed everything. Today, the author writes and publishes with regularity and has fun in the process.

This resource is filled with first-time writer help and creative tools for established authors. You will learn numerous writing strategies based on proven principles. Learn them fast, develop your writing habit, and become an elite writer who publishes with consistency. This resource is ideal for writers searching for fresh tools, authors who want to write more often and anyone who longs to write a book.

Get this resource here:

https://www.amazon.com/dp/B07NBQHCF F/

18) *Self-Discipline for Writers*
Writing Is Hard, But You Too Can Write and Publish Books Regularly

by Martin Meadows

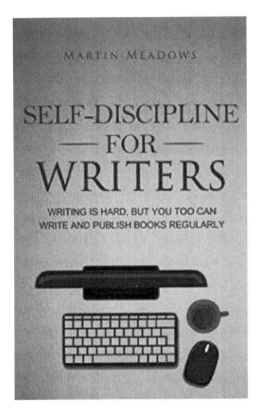

RESOURCE OVERVIEW

In this book, a top-selling author shares his strategies and philosophy on how to cultivate self-discipline as a writer and keep writing every day for years to come.

You will discover:

- The keys to self-discipline for writers
- How to avoid a common mistake that lead to failure
- How to develop a strong work ethic to help you consistently hit your word counts
- How to overcome common kinds of self-doubt among writers
- How to manage your energy as a writer to meet your goals
- Profitable business practices for more self-discipline

Writing does not have to be hard. You too can do it with more ease, publish consistently and earn more money with the tips in this book.

Get this resource here:

https://www.amazon.com/dp/B07RDXCHBK/

19) *Writing Tools*
55 Essential Strategies for Every Writer

by Roy Peter Clark

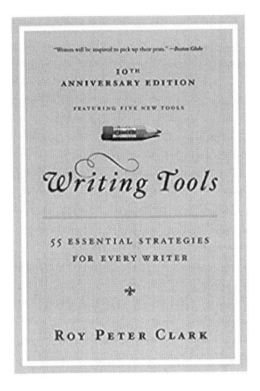

RESOURCE OVERVIEW

In this special edition of Clark's top-selling guide to writing:

A decade ago, the United States' most influential writing teacher leveraged nearly three decades of experience in journalism, teaching and writing to craft a series of fifty brief essays on varying aspects of writing. In the past ten years, the book has become a classic guide for experts and novices, making it one of the most loved resources on writing.

Broken down into four sections, the book includes more than 200 examples from literature and journalism. This newest edition also includes five new, never-before-seen tools.

Accessible, inspiring, entertaining and useful for any type of writer, from novelists to high school students, this book is essential reading.

Get this resource here:

https://www.amazon.com/dp/B000SEIW9E/

20) *Time Management for Writers*

How to write faster, find the time to write your book, and be a more prolific writer

by Sandra Gerth

RESOURCE OVERVIEW

In the modern digital age, publishing is easier than most would have ever dreamed. Unfortunately, finding the time to actually write a book is not so easy. With family obligations, day jobs, household duties, and valued hobbies, most writers struggle to get much writing done.

Readers and publishers expect authors to create numerous books each year, while also finding time to market each book through social media, blogging and networking.

If you're one of the many writers who is struggling to find the time to write, this resource is for you.

Get this resource here:

https://www.amazon.com/dp/B01950TAO2/

ESSENTIAL APPS FOR WRITERS

#1 *SelfControl*

OVERVIEW

Available for Mac OS X, Cost: Free

Everyone knows how easy it is to lose focus with temptations, such as internet distractions, textas and notifications from social media.. As a writer, you must focus to free up your creativity. If you have a tendency to check Facebook every 15 minutes, this app is a life-saver.

If you can't control yourself, SelfControl will do the job for you by blocking your ability to access a list of sites of your choosing for a specified time period. This way, all you have no choice but to sit and be productive. Even if you delete this app or restart your computer, once you click, there will be no way to access the blocked websites until the time you specify.

Get the app at:

https://selfcontrolapp.com/

#2 *Hemingway*

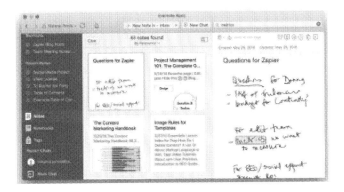

OVERVIEW

Available for web browser, cost: free

We all make spelling and grammatical mistakes at some point. This app highlights common grammatical errors and lengthy, complex sentences, using colored that make the needed corrections crystal clear.

Every word counts for a professional writer. Unnecessary words add confusion, make your look less professional and devalue your writing. If you need maximum clarity, this is a great tool.

Get the app at:

http://www.hemingwayapp.com/

#3 *Evernote*

OVERVIEW

Available for Android and iOS, cost: free

This app lets you create-to-do-lists, save information and take note wherever and whenever an idea pops into your mind, create-to-do-lists, and save things you find online into Evernote.

It can be a game-changer for writers who want to retain information and get work done. The app also makes it easy to share content on social media like Twitter, Facebook and LinkedIn, or save URLs to clipboard. It also automatically syncs all updates and content between your tablet, phone and computer.

Get the app at:

https://evernote.com/download

#4 *Write or Die*

OVERVIEW

Available for iOS, cost: $9, 99

This app will help push you past your writer's block by applying real-world consequences if you decide to procrastinate.

The "bad things: rangefrom a disapproving cat staring you down to disastrous consequences with a terrifying Kamikaze mode. The app also includes a Reward Mode which gives you perks when you complete a specified number of words.

Get the app at:

https://v2.writeordie.com/

#5 *Story Tracker*

Story Tracker
Writer's Submission Tracking
Andrew Nicolle
★★★★★ 4.4 • 5 Ratings
$7.99

Screenshots iPhone iPad

OVERVIEW

Available for iOS, cost: $8, 99

A valuable tool for freelancers, this app makes it easy to keep track of your submitted stories, articles, poems, novels, poems and scripts. Many journals, magazines and other markets forbid simultaneous submissions.

It can be easy to forget where you have actually submitted your work when you have to deal with hundreds of articles or stories. In addition to tracking your submissions, you can view the total money earned for every piece and add details for every market, including title, editor, genre and deadline.

Get the app at:

https://apps.apple.com/us/app/story-tracker/id326115341

#6 *The Brainstormer*

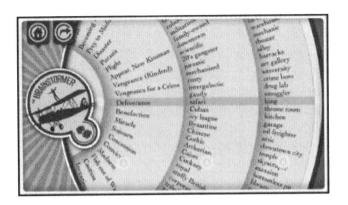

OVERVIEW

Available for: iOS, Cost: $1, 99

Writing is difficult., especially when you have to deal with the dreaded writer's block. This app helps you spark new ideas, overcome creative blocks and quickly come up with subjects for sketching. doodling or journaling.

By doing a random spin or manipulating the app's wheels, you can generate combinations that make incredible creative writing prompts. Even if you don't end up using the suggested scenario, it can help you come up with brilliant storylines and inspire your creativity.

Get the app at:

https://www.tapnik.com/brainstormer/

#7 *Mind Node*

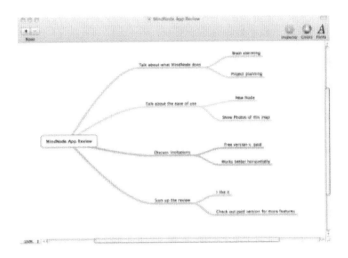

OVERVIEW

Available for: iOS, Cost: $9, 99

    This mind-mapping app generates visual representations of your bright ideas. It helps you brainstorm, share and organize your thoughts in a very intuitive way. The app's clean interface lets you generate and link big and complicated thoughts together.

    Seeing your ideas makes it much easier to connect unrelated topics. This app also lets you highlight, color code and customize the branches.

Get the app at:

https://mindnode.com/

#8 *List for Writers*

OVERVIEW

Available for: iOS and Android, Cost: $2, 99

If you have trouble generating new ideas, this app is a godsend. It delivers list after list of ideas and writing prompts, including names, plot lines, character traits, occupations, action verbs, obsessions and much more. The app also offers dictionary support and a notepad feature that lets you collect lists and notes.

Get the app at:

https://play.google.com/store/apps/details?id=com.thinkamingo.listsforwriters&hl=en_US

#9 *Hanx Writer*

OVERVIEW

Only available on the App Store for iOS devices.

Famous actor Tom Hanks produced the quirky Hanx Writer, a cool little app which turns your smartphone into a old-school typewriter, complete with dings and clacks. You can cut, create, paste and share docs.

You can also turn off the option so you can delete text, just like with an actual typewriter. The actor's tribute to a bygone era, this app is a fun way to enhance your smartphone experience.

Get the app at:

http://hanxwriter.com/

#10 *Scrivener*

OVERVIEW

Available for: iOS and Android,

The go-to app for every level of writer, Scrivener is used every day by screenwriters, best-selling novelists, non-fiction writers, academics, students, lawyers, translators, journalists and more.

The app won't tell you how you should write; but it will provide everything you need to begin writing and keep writing great stuff.

Get the app at:

https://www.literatureandlatte.com/scrivener/overview

HELPFUL RESOURCE FOR AUTHORS

If you're an author trying to sell more books, we at Writing Axis have created the following resource to help you use Amazon Marketing (AMS) to get more readers,

Get 40,000 effective keywords you can copy and paste into your AMS campaigns

This resource includes:

- Tips on how to use Amazon Marketing more effectively to reduce the cost of advertising and make more readers aware of your book
- 40,000 effective keyword phrases you can quickly copy and paste directly into your AMS campaigns

- A convenient FAQ to help you leverage these 40,000 keywords and a clickable table of contents to help you navigate the resource
- Detailed information on how to copy and paste from this Kindle book to a Word doc or directly into your AMS campaigns

Available at Amazon at

https://www.amazon.com/dp/B07ZWBXCW3

10 SITES THAT PAY FOR CREATIVE WRITING

There are several sites that will pay very good money for short stories, poetry and other types of creative writing. Some of our favorites include:

#1 - AGNI

AGNI is Boston University's literary magazine. They will pay you for critical essays, short contemporary fiction and poetry.

You can only submit from September to May each year.

Expect to earn $20 per each page of poetry and $10 per every printed page of fiction. You will also get a free year's subscription to the magazine.

Get all the details here:

https://agnionline.bu.edu/

#2 - BWR

The graduate English department magazine for the U of Alabama, Black Warrior Review is published twice a year.

While they look for contemporary fiction, futuristic stories and magical realism are encouraged, as long as the stories push boundaries and encourage deep thought.

Expect to earn a nice lump sum for a published story, although the exact amount isn't something they typically publicize.

Get all the details here:

https://bwr.ua.edu/

#3 - *Boulevard*

This award-winning journal pay for contemporary short stories, essays and poetry.

It particularly likes new, unpublished writers over accomplished writers who have already been published.

Although it doesn't accept genre fiction, Boulevard will pay from $25 to$250 for poetry and $100 to $300 for good prose.

Get all the details here:

https://boulevardmagazine.org/

#4 - *Carve*

Carve will pay $100 per short story for its website. It also has a print magazine that will publish nonfiction, poetry and illustrations.

Editors often take the time to respond to submissions with polite, thoughtful editorial critiques.

Carve only publishes quality literary fiction, so don't submit genre fiction, such as horror, thrillers, fantasy, sci-fi, romance, etc.)

Get all the details here:

https://www.carvezine.com/

#5 - *Glimmertrain*

Glimmertrain champions emerging new writers by paying $700 and up for each accepted story.

Check the site to find out what they're currently looking for.

Categories usually include super-short fiction and diverse topical themes. You also have a chance to make thousands of dollars by entering your work in contests.

Get all the details here:

http://www.glimmertrain.org/

#6 - *The Iowa Review*

Part of the U of Iowa writing program, this famous journal has been paying writers since 1970.

It looks for poetry, fiction and creative nonfiction in a wide array of styles.

The journal only accepts submissions from September to November each year.

Expect to earn $0.80 per word for all fiction work, with at least a $100 payment.

Get all the details here:

https://iowareview.org/

#7 - *Threepenny Review*

Threepenny Review will pay you for poetry, contemporary literary fiction and a diversity of essays and other types of nonfiction.

It only publishes four times a year both online and in print.

Expect to earn $200 for poems and $400 for short stories.

Get all the details here:

http://threepennyreview.com/

#8 - *The Southern Review*

The Southern Review pays for poetry, contemporary fiction and select nonfiction including book reviews and essays.

The magazine only accepts submissions from September to December.

Expect to make $25 per page, with a set maximum of $200. You will also get a year's subscription if your writing is accepted.

Get all the details here:

https://thesouthernreview.org/

#9 - Ploughshares

Ploughshares will pay $25 per page for contemporary literary fiction.

There's a minimum payout of $50 and a set maximum payout of $250.

The journal also has a yearly Emerging Writers Contest for self-published writers and previously unpublished authors.

Get all the details here:

https://www.pshares.org/

#10 - *The Missouri Review*

THE MISSOURI REVIEW

This journal pays well for poetry, contemporary fiction and nonfiction essays.

Publishing since 1978, The Missouri Review frequently accepts work from new writers.

Expect t0o make $40 per printed page if they like your writing.

Get all the details here:

https://www.missourireview.com/

Made in the USA
Coppell, TX
07 February 2020

15513949R00122